Step Out Of Debt into Wealth in 10 Steps

KEJI ADEBESHIN

contents

disclaimer

I am not a certified financial advisor. I am an ordinary person on an extraordinary journey. I seek to learn the language of money and share the ways that I have made it work for me in the hopes of helping others.

This e-book does not constitute personal financial advice. Please seek independent financial advice appropriate to your financial situation from a registered and qualified legal or financial practitioner.

FOR WOMEN, FINANCIAL INDEPENDENCE IS A MATTER OF NECESSITY.

CARRIE SCHWAB-POMERANTZ
BOARD CHAIR AND PRESIDENT, *CHARLES SCHWAB FOUNDATION*

synopsis

Let me start by saying **thank you** for investing in this e-book. I hope you are as excited to read it as I was to write it!

Financial literacy and money management are topics that are simply not talked about enough in today's society. Being able to successfully manage our income is key to financial stability for ourselves and our families. So, I've made it my mission to share all that I have learnt about money - and continue to learn - with women worldwide.

This e-book is a beginner's guide to spending less, saving more and paying down debt. I'll introduce you to 10 important steps that you can take to gradually pay down debt and invest on the side. These steps have helped me too.

With these steps, supported by the budget tracker provided, you'll be able to embark on a successful financial journey. You will be able to track where your money goes and reach savings and investment goals you set for yourself.

So sit back, relax and happy reading!

All my love,
Keji xx

MY JOURNEY FROM DEBT TO WEALTH

If I could pretend I'm a character from *Mission Impossible,* hopping back and forth between rooftops, with the corners of my mouth extending almost as far as my earlobes, hollering: *"I'm on my way! I'm doing it! I can't believe I'm doing it!* Yes!"I would.

The ultimate financial rabbit-hole is bad debt. It's easy to get into, but harder to get out of. In fact, you don't just jump out, you dig through for a long period of time, digging and digging, until you finally crawl your way out. Unless you are already a multi-millionaire, YouTube superstar, or win the lottery, climbing out of debt is hard. Even so, getting rid of it takes a good amount of effort, and once it's gone? Close friends have described the feeling as "liberating", "freeing".

The tips within this e-book are intended to set you on a path to financial freedom. My ultimate pride and joy would be this e-book making an impact in your own financial journey. To begin, please allow me tell you a bit about the inspiration behind the book.

I officially embarked on my money journey in March 2019. This was mostly prompted by my spontaneous move out of our family home in New Zealand in my late 20s, to one of the most expensive cities in the world - Sydney, Australia. For the first time in my life, I was on my own. And, I needed to survive.

With newfound independence came the determination to learn the language of money. In order for me to fully embrace a "new beginning", I needed to be real with the state of my finances. I was $53,073 deep in student loan debt, which would begin to accrue 4% interest a year later due to the move. I also had $27,769 (interest included) in business loans spread across three credit cards and one family loan, a $3,063 travel loan, and a $2,740 rental bond - an exact total of $86,645.82 (NZD) hanging over my head.

I knew I had to get rid of these for a fresh start, all the while paying rent, unending bills, vehicle expenses, and fostering a social life in a new country. This was that moment where I wished a fairy godmother would appear out of nowhere, flick her exquisitely decorated wand and magically whisk the debts away. Who was I kidding, right? I needed to make a change, and I needed to start NOW.

Fast-forward to May 2020...

As at the time of writing this e-book, 14 months has gone by. I am happy to report that I am no longer merely surviving, I'm thriving. I developed a highly effective money management process (i.e. the 10 steps we'll discuss) and have cultivated various habits that have enabled me to spend less and save more.

I have successfully managed to knock down my mountain of debt by 30% with "gazelle intensity" (in the words of financial personality, Dave Ramsey). It might not seem much to some, but paying off $26,286 in debt within a span of 14 months is something anyone should be proud of. I've also been building an emergency fund and investing in stocks and peer-to-peer lending on the side. According to my documented money plan, based on my current gross income, I will debt-free by mid-2022, if not earlier.

So, you can see why if I could pretend I'm a character from *Mission Impossible,* hopping back and forth between rooftops, with the corners of my mouth extending almost as far as my earlobes, hollering: *"I'm on my way! I'm doing it! I can't believe I'm doing it! Yes!*" I would.

The 10 steps you are about to learn have helped me spend less and save more. They are practical and achievable, and if I can achieve all that I have achieved money-wise, I have absolute faith that you can too.

NOW, IT'S YOUR TURN

Before we get into it all, I'd just like to ask - are you ready? Are you ready to turn things around? Are you ready to pay off that loan? Build an investment portfolio? Save for a house? Build an emergency fund? Invest in your future?

If so, just say to yourself, "I'm ready".

Why am I asking you this? Well, simply put - embarking on this journey is not easy. I can tell you this first-hand and you probably know it too. Money is elusive. It comes and goes as it pleases. It's like a radical yo-yo with loose strings. Money is so hard to pin down that I had to create a system to help me manage it. This is the same system I will to introduce to you shortly.

By the end of this e-book, you should be equipped with the tools to fix the strings. You will be able to control where your money goes, when and how often. At the end of it all, you should be able to keep more of it in your pockets.

So, let's begin with Step #1...

STEP 1: CUT THAT CREDIT CARD - LIKE, RIGHT NOW

We're breaking up with our credit cards. Yes - you heard that right. Cut it up, right now. Why? Because the relationship is toxic. It's not making our finances better. It's not bringing out the best part of us. The best we know we can be. The best we *want* to be. But wait, before you slice that piece of plastic into pieces, let's talk about the concept of "debt" and credit cards for a minute.

When I started my money journey early 2019, the very first move I made was to cut up the only two physical credit cards I had. This was a turning point for me - the very act of breaking my financial lifeline made my journey very *real.*

The credit cards were not serving me, *I* was serving *them.* I was serving the bank. But, not anymore.

> Cutting them up was a symbolic moment being that I would no longer have a choice but to rely on my own hard-earned money.
>
> AUTHOR'S NOTE

Cutting them up was a symbolic moment, being that I would no longer have a choice but to rely on my own hard-earned money. I would no longer have a choice but to be wiser in how I spent from there onwards.

“

CREDIT CARDS ARE LIKE THAT GUY WE JUST HAD TO DATE IN HIGH SCHOOL. YOU KNOW THE ONE: HE WAS HANDSOME, BRAZEN, AND DROVE A SUPER-CHARGED MUSTANG (OR MAYBE A MOTORCYCLE!). IT WAS FUN WHILE IT LASTED. BUT IT ENDED IN HEARTBREAK, AS WE KNEW IT WOULD.

KRISTIN DELFAU
AUTHOR, *TURBO-MOM'S GUIDE TO SAVING MONEY WITHOUT WASTING TIME* (2009)

There are many conflicting opinions in the financial community about credit cards. To have it or not to have it is literally the question. The people who defend credit cards will tell you that it's great for your credit score! You'll love yourself for having one because if you were to ever to borrow money, you won't have to pay as high in interest. They'll even tell you that not paying huge interest is literally *saving* you money. And that's our goal, right?

Meanwhile, those who absolutely hate credit cards will tell you to stay far away. They'll say that borrowing someone else's money is basically asking for sleepless nights and constant headaches. It's easy to get, hard to pay back. Not only that, some people can rely on debt too much and keep overspending. Buying that luxury car that could take them years to pay back, with interest. Or booking that cruise that though will be over in a flash, the debt will still hang around. Like an annoying pest.

Both parties aren't wrong. But, the fact remains - while credit scores are mightily important, having debt by definition is basically borrowing from your future earnings. Part of your future income belongs to the people you owe. Hello, sleepless nights? And, credit cards are the ultimate vehicles of debt - why? Because of their ridiculously high interest rates.

From the above, we can deduce that debt is both a burden and an opportunity - depending on how you use it. So, the keyword here is *discipline.*

How disciplined are you with your credit card? Do you spend under the limit? Do you pay back your balances on time? Are you making use of the money-saving rewards that comes with it like airfare points, cashbacks, shopping gift cards, and so on? Is it *actually* building your credit score? If so, you're doing it right.

Say you currently have some loans to pay back and you have a credit card at the same time. Is your credit card saving/ making you money, or are you losing money? If you're losing money, it's time to let it go.

> ...is your credit card saving/ making you money, or are you losing money?

AUTHOR'S NOTE

You simply cannot pay back debt while losing money. That's like trying to fill a bucket with a hole in it. We need to seal that hole. We need to keep more money to be able to have more money to pay our debts with. This is why so many of us run into deficit (i.e. negative back account balances). We spend more than we can afford, and expect to pay off loans on time.

Hypothetically, if you only had $300 in your account to survive for a month, with no line of credit, wouldn't you get creative and begin to find ways to ration how you spend it? Yes, you will. You will begin to find ways to save on purchases you may have otherwise overlooked had you had a credit card.

Bottom line - if you want to keep credit cards, do make sure you're using it to work *for* you and not against you. If it's working against you, cut it up right now. To save *your* money, the first step is to cut ties with *someone else's* money - at least until you're at the stage where you can comfortably use someone else's money to make more money.

So decide now - to cut or not to cut that credit card? That is your question.

I HAVE DECIDED THAT:

....

SO THAT:

....

“

CREATING WEALTH COMES DOWN TO DISCIPLINE.

ALLISON VANASKI
SENIOR FINANCIAL PLANNER,
ARCADIA WEALTH MANAGEMENT

STEP 2: CREATE YOUR PERSONAL BUDGET

Sitting down to type a budget might actually be one of the most boring and time-consuming tasks on the planet. At least to me! But, it's undoubtedly the most important thing we need to do. Once it's done, that's when the fun begins.

If you could take just one thing away from this book, it's this one. Step 2. Hands down. Why? Because creating a budget sets the foundation for all your money decisions. Day or night, it's the lamp that lights the path to successfully managing where your money goes.

With a budget, not only do you see clearly how you spend your money, you also see the various ways you can save money. Saving money adds more money to your bottom line (that is, how much you have left over after you account for all outgoings).

P.S: I interchange "bottom line" with "net income" throughout this e-book.

So, how do you create a budget?

There are so many apps out there that can help. Some popular ones are Mint, You Need A Budget (YNAB), and PocketBook. These can populate your figures and even track your expenses for you. They are handy on-the-go if you need to refer to your numbers. Your bank may also provide budgeting tools. These are great at integrating your account movements with your budget goals.

Another suggestion is using a good ol' Microsoft Excel spreadsheet - I prefer this method and it's what I use to this day. I'm a big believer in finding the simplest, least costly and most efficient way of doing things. This is what *My Freedom Plan* (MFP) budget tracker is for. But before we get into that, see below a very condensed version of the tracker. It's the basic budget template you'll see anywhere.

Gross Income:	$XXX
Monthly Bills (45% of Gross Income):	$XXX (*Rent + Phone + Internet + Electricity & Gas + Hot Water + Petrol + Groceries + Tithe + Insurance)*
Debt Repayment (30% of Gross Income):	$XXX
Savings (10% of Gross Income):	$XXX
Net Income (15% of Gross Income):	$XXX

This is my actual monthly outgoings in a snapshot. You'll get to replace the triple X with your own numbers shortly.

You will notice I split each category into percentages. This is good practice as it helps you to stay the course and be consistent month after month. There will be months when the percentages change slightly. For example, you may decide to put less towards Debt Repayment and more towards Savings depending on your goals for that month. Nevertheless, try your best to maintain the percentages you set for yourself from the start. Don't squeeze yourself too hard, otherwise your plan may not be sustainable. Set percentages that you are comfortable with and are realistic.

Now onto the MFP budget tracker. This tracker is the bigger picture. It's much more in-depth as it'll contain not only these categories, but also a monthly breakdown of your outgoings. This spreadsheet will guide you every step of the way on your financial journey. Call me crazy, but you should treat it like a personal friend! You'll be able to track all your debt repayments, savings and investments on a regular basis. This way, you can see how far you ve come and how far you have to go.

...try your best to maintain the percentages you set for yourself from the start.

AUTHOR'S NOTE

I'm a visual and systematic person, hence why I designed the spreadsheet in a 'big picture - drill down' type format. I personally refer to it every week and it has helped me a lot to stay on track. I'm sharing it with you because it can help you too.

If you would like to download the full template for your own personal use, please visit sisterswithaplan.com. It's a very useful tool to have and it's free. As you read the remaining steps below, you'll understand better how to use it. Then, you can truly be confident in your journey from debt to wealth.

ACTION PLAN

Work out the percentage of your bills per month (p/m)

RECURRING EXPENSES	COST PER MONTH
....	....
....	....
....	....
....	....
....	....

TOTAL COST P/M: ....

GROSS INCOME P/M: .... % OF MONTHLY BILLS: ....

STEP 3: START BUILDING AN EMERGENCY FUND

Imagine that you had been taking all the steps to spend less and save more, using your savings to pay down debt and perhaps invest on the side, only to get slammed with an unexpected traffic fine of $400 that has to be paid before your next pay day. What would you do?

You wouldn't reach for your credit card because oops, you cut that into pieces some weeks ago. Even if you didn't, you don't want to have more debt on your plate if you use it. You could consider getting a payday loan or loan from family or friend - but that'll put you in more debt, basically undermining all the progress you'd made towards debt repayment.

You could consider using part of your 15% net income, but you would frown at the opportunity cost that comes with it. (Opportunity cost is the cost of spending money on something that otherwise could've been spent on something else worthwhile during that period.) Even worse: What if you had $200 left in your net income for the rest of that month? This is certainly not enough to pay a $400 fine.

Indeed, our brains would be busy trying to figure out several ways to pay this unexpected expense. This is where an emergency fund - the *Superman* of personal finance -comes to the rescue! Receiving the $400 fine would first annoy you (of course), but then bring a peace of mind like no other when you realise you have funds stashed away in an obscure, but liquid, bank account. ("Liquid" means it's easy to take your money out if you need it.) You'll simply pull funds from your emergency fund to pay the fine, then go on your merry way.

With an emergency fund, unexpected expenses would no longer be a burden, but an inconvenience with a quick fix. Think of an emergency fund this way - it is your own bank. You need money, you lend yourself some money, then you return it at your own pace, with no interest or penalties. Events that I have had to access my emergency fund for in the past year have been rental bond and vehicle-related expenses including a traffic fine (yes, that was a true story), registration renewal, and license renewal. Life happens, but you should not have to struggle to get back on track.

With an emergency fund, unexpected expenses would no longer be a burden, but an inconvenience with a quick fix.

AUTHOR'S NOTE

How much should you have in your emergency fund?

The better question is: How much would you be comfortable with sitting in your emergency fund? Assuming, God forbid, you lose your job today, how much money would you need to sustain your basic needs for the next three months until you find another source of income? That's how much should sit in your emergency fund.

I personally allocate a certain amount to my emergency fund every month. I don't skip a month. I will stop when I have enough to cover me for a year's worth. So, if you haven't already, figure out your number and start to build an emergency fund. Find the best bank that offers a high interest savings account with no minimum deposit and no withdraw limits and penalties. In Australia, AMP Saver Account tops my list. Do find something similar in your own country.

ACTION PLAN

Work out how much you need to save for emergencies

Monthly expenses total (from Step 2): ....

Multiply by 3 months = ... should be saved, at least

Multiply by 6 months = ... should be saved, at least

Multiply by 12 months = ... should be saved, at least

WHATEVER YOU WANT TO DO, IF YOU WANT TO BE GREAT AT IT, YOU HAVE TO LOVE IT AND BE ABLE TO MAKE SACRIFICES FOR IT.

MAYA ANGELOU, RENOWNED POET

STEP 4: HAVE A DAILY SPEND LIMIT

So, you have cut up your credit card, worked out your recurring expenses and planned an emergency fund system, congratulations! You are on your way towards putting more money in your pockets at the end of every month.

For me, having a daily spend limit was the key to successfully managing my net income each month, especially in the first few months. Simply put, I would divide my net income across the number of days in that month (e.g. 30 days), then have a per day limit I can spend. For example, if I had $800 in net income to last me for a monthly pay cycle, I would divide $800 by 30 days which equals to $26.66 per day. This basically meant that I could not spend more than $26.66 per day.

The best part was realising that even before my money journey, I didn't spend every day anyway. This meant that now, the spend limit amount from the previous day could roll over into the next day totalling, for example, $53.32 ($26.66 x 2). This then meant that I had even more money to play with that day if I choose to spend it.

This is a fun exercise and I highly recommend it, especially if you're a spontaneous shopper who would like to keep better track of your weekly expenditure. Nobody likes to run out of funds before their next income hits. Below is the template that I update on Microsoft Word once a month. I print this out and pin it on the $12 cork board I bought from Kmart Australia. P.S: Cork boards are so underrated!

	June 2019 Budget: $600						
	Monday	Tuesday	Wednesday	Thursday	Friday	Saturday	Sunday
$40						15 LIMIT: $20 SPENT: ____ BAL: ______	16 LIMIT: $20 SPENT: ____ BAL: ______
$140	17 LIMIT: $20 SPENT: ____ BAL: ______	18 LIMIT: $20 SPENT: ____ BAL: ______	19 LIMIT: $20 SPENT: ____ BAL: ______	20 LIMIT: $20 SPENT: ____ BAL: ______	21 LIMIT: $20 SPENT: ____ BAL: ______	22 LIMIT: $20 SPENT: ____ BAL: ______	23 LIMIT: $20 SPENT: ____ BAL: ______
$140	24 LIMIT: $20 SPENT: ____ BAL: ______	25 LIMIT: $20 SPENT: ____ BAL: ______	26 LIMIT: $20 SPENT: ____ BAL: ______	27 LIMIT: $20 SPENT: ____ BAL: ______	28 LIMIT: $20 SPENT: ____ BAL: ______	29 LIMIT: $20 SPENT: ____ BAL: ______	30 LIMIT: $20 SPENT: ____ BAL: ______
$140	1 LIMIT: $20 SPENT: ____ BAL: ______	2 LIMIT: $20 SPENT: ____ BAL: ______	3 LIMIT: $20 SPENT: ____ BAL: ______	4 LIMIT: $20 SPENT: ____ BAL: ______	5 LIMIT: $20 SPENT: ____ BAL: ______	6 LIMIT: $20 SPENT: ____ BAL: ______	7 LIMIT: $20 SPENT: ____ BAL: ______
$140	8 LIMIT: $20 SPENT: ____ BAL: ______	9 LIMIT: $20 SPENT: ____ BAL: ______	10 LIMIT: $20 SPENT: ____ BAL: ______	11 LIMIT: $20 SPENT: ____ BAL: ______	12 LIMIT: $20 SPENT: ____ BAL: ______	13 LIMIT: $20 SPENT: ____ BAL: ______	14 LIMIT: $20 SPENT: ____ BAL: ______

At the top is the Month, Year, and Budget amount. The calendar starts on pay day through to the day before the next pay day. In the cells, you'll write your daily limit, how much you've spent (or not spent) that day, and the Balance. On the left-hand side is your weekly total. That's all! Simple and easy.

Visit sisterswithaplan.com to download the free template for your own use.

I LEARNED TO ALWAYS TAKE ON THINGS I'D NEVER DONE BEFORE. GROWTH AND COMFORT DO NOT COEXIST.

VIRGINIA ROMETTY
CEO, *IBM*

STEP 5: DEVELOP AND *MAINTAIN* A GROWTH MINDSET

As I mentioned earlier, the path to financial freedom is not easy. If it were, we'd all be millionaires. Think of a time in your life when you had a goal and you stopped at nothing to achieve it. I bet you achieved it! This is exactly the same attitude we should adopt to see our money journey through. Whether you have $5,000 in credit card debt or a $100,000 in student loan fees, debt is debt, and paying it off won't be a walk in the park. In saying that, though, it is entirely doable as long as we learn how to manoeuvre our money to do the right thing.

I can't imagine achieving all that I have achieved in life without being persistent. It's one thing to have the desire and drive to do something, it's another thing to maintain that drive. I started from zero dollars, and I was able to save my first $2,000 emergency fund, pay $26,286 in debt, and start an investment portfolio, all within a span of a year and two months. Let me tell you three ways that I have been able to maintain my drive that you may find useful.

Firstly, have a financial mantra. At the very top of my budget tracker is a money mantra that stays top of mind on my journey. It reads, "Acquire money, keep money, put money to work". This is an idea I wrote down while reading one of my favourite money books titled *The Richest Man in Babylon* by George S. Clason. Although written 94 years ago, this book is still as relevant as ever. It's changed many people's lives (based on the testimonials online) and I suggest you read it if you haven't already. It's a great introduction to understanding the rules of money and putting it into practice. If you can't get a physical copy, you can listen to the free audiobook. like I did. This mantra that I wrote down has been guiding my money decisions ever since.

I also have a mantra for my savings activity. Also from *The Richest Man in Babylon*, I jotted down the quote: "A part of what I earn is mine to keep". Clason suggests saving 10% of your gross income (you will notice this is where I got my percentage in Step 2 from). If in one month I need to shuffle some percentages around, I always go back to this mantra to ensure I save at least 10%, regardless. I'll do myself a disservice if I don't.

BOOK SUGGESTION

The second way you can maintain momentum is doing what you're doing now: consuming content about financial freedom. Thanks to the Internet, there are so many resources out there now. As often as you can, read financial e-books, library books, audiobooks, watch YouTube videos, sign up for financial programs like Dave Ramsey's *Financial Peace University,* read investing blogs, and be involved in anything else that'll inspire you. You'll learn something new every day and it'll keep you motivated and energised. Just like you, there are many others looking to make money work for them and not the other way round.

Fortunately, there are so many people out there willing to help! If all of this sounds overwhelming, start small. Get on YouTube.com and find new financial education channels to follow.

The final way you can maintain my growth mindset is simply imagining the future you'd love to have. The future where you and your family can live comfortably. The future where you don't have to seek permission from work months in advance to attend family functions and important milestones. The future where you work because you *want* to not because you *have* to. The future where you set your own schedule and are able to occupy yourself with philanthropic projects and other hobbies of interest. This future is my bigger picture.

What's your bigger picture? Right now, in the worksheet on the next page, write down five components of your "bigger picture". Be as specific as possible.

MY BIGGER PICTURE IS A FUTURE WHEREBY I:

1. ....
2. ....
3. ....
4. ....
5. ....

How good, and slightly terrifying, does that feel? Don't be terrified, it's possible!

Now, why don't you develop your own mantra too? Your mantra should motivate you and keep you in check at all times. It should also link very closely to your financial goals.

MY MONEY MANTRA IS:

....

....

....

....

"

YOU'VE GOT TO VISUALIZE WHERE YOU'RE HEADED AND BE VERY CLEAR ABOUT IT. TAKE A POLAROID PICTURE OF WHERE YOU'RE GOING TO BE IN A FEW YEARS.

FOUNDER, *SPANX*

STEP 6: HAVE A 5-YEAR FINANCIAL PLAN

Remember how I said my budget tracker (the MFP tracker) was more in-depth than simply tracking my gross income, outgoings and net income? If you have downloaded the template already, you'll notice two sections of the budget - Debt Repayment and Investments. If not, don't worry, keep reading, it will still make sense.

On the first column, you'll notice that there are 60 months in chronological order (5 years). The Debt Repayment section is where you would list each debt you need to pay off each month or fortnightly. The Investment section is where you would list each investment you want to send money to each month or fortnightly.

Tracking Debt Repayments

Let's run through this section first. See example, using the budget tracker, on the next page.

TRACKING DEBT REPAYMENT

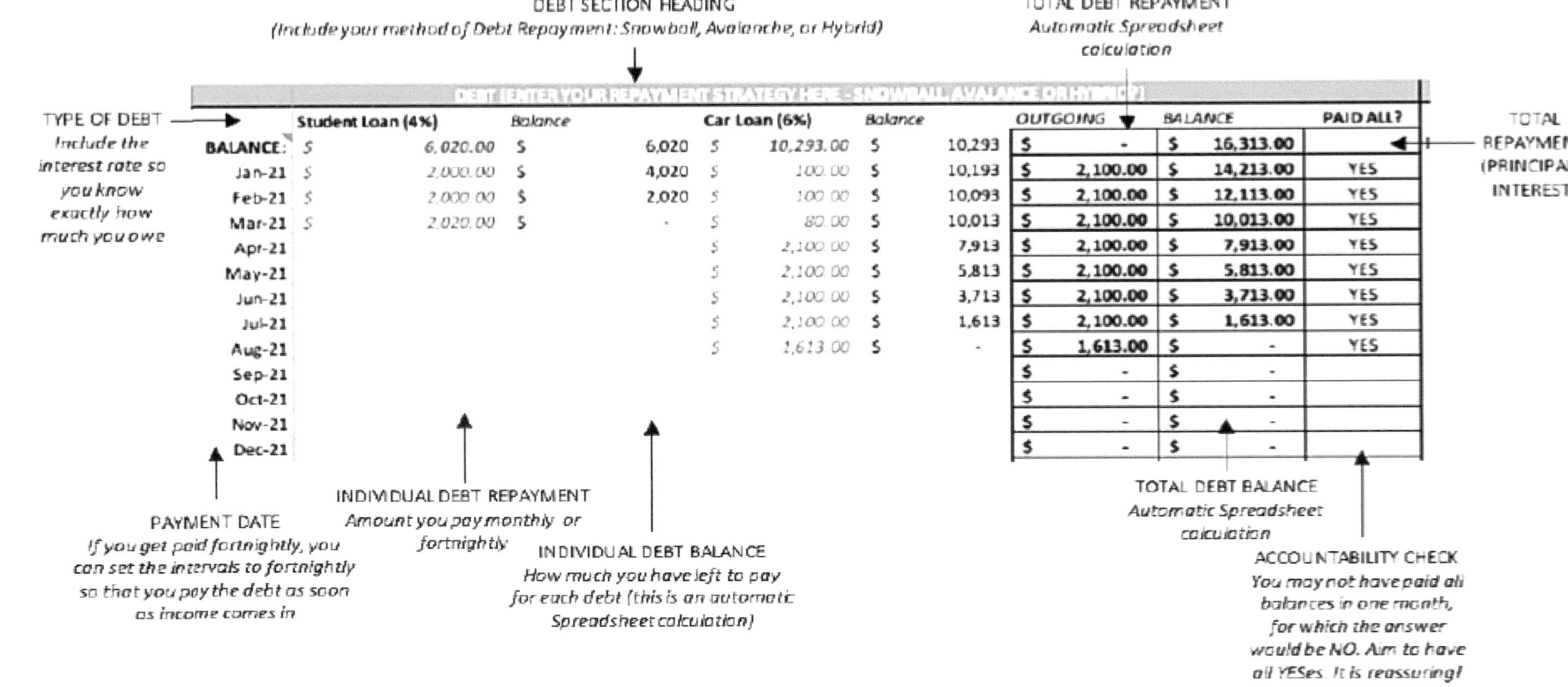

DEBT (ENTER YOUR REPAYMENT STRATEGY HERE - SNOWBALL, AVALANCE OR HYBRID?)

	Student Loan (4%)	Balance	Car Loan (6%)	Balance	OUTGOING	BALANCE	PAID ALL?
BALANCE:	$ 6,020.00	$ 6,020	$ 10,293.00	$ 10,293	$ -	$ 16,313.00	
Jan-21	$ 2,000.00	$ 4,020	$ 100.00	$ 10,193	$ 2,100.00	$ 14,213.00	YES
Feb-21	$ 2,000.00	$ 2,020	$ 100.00	$ 10,093	$ 2,100.00	$ 12,113.00	YES
Mar-21	$ 2,020.00	$ -	$ 80.00	$ 10,013	$ 2,100.00	$ 10,013.00	YES
Apr-21			$ 2,100.00	$ 7,913	$ 2,100.00	$ 7,913.00	YES
May-21			$ 2,100.00	$ 5,813	$ 2,100.00	$ 5,813.00	YES
Jun-21			$ 2,100.00	$ 3,713	$ 2,100.00	$ 3,713.00	YES
Jul-21			$ 2,100.00	$ 1,613	$ 2,100.00	$ 1,613.00	YES
Aug-21			$ 1,613.00	$ -	$ 1,613.00	$ -	YES
Sep-21					$ -	$ -	
Oct-21					$ -	$ -	
Nov-21					$ -	$ -	
Dec-21					$ -	$ -	

In order to fill in your numbers, go back to your percentage. What percentage of your Gross Income can you allocate towards debt repayment? Once you get this percentage, determine what your debt payment method is (Snowball, Avalanche, or Hybrid). Then, allocate monthly/fortnightly numbers to each debt.

If you haven't heard of these debt payment methods before, I'll quickly explain it.

The snowball method pays off the smallest of your debts. Say you have a $5,000 and a $2,000 loan. Using the snowball method, you would pay off the $2,000 first before the $5,000 loan. If your $5,000 loan has a minimum monthly payment on it, you'll pay the minimum payment while sending more of your money to tackle the $2,000 loan. That's basically it.

The only thing is the snowball method doesn't consider interest rates. If your $2,000 debt only has a 2% interest rate per annum and your $5,000 loan is at a whopping 27% p.a., you'll definitely pay more overall using the snowball method. Of course, this depends on how long you take to pay off the $2,000. The longer you take, the more interest your $5,000 loan accrues. So, what some do is choose the avalanche method instead.

The avalanche method would pay off your loan with the highest interest rate while you pay the minimum on the other debts. So, in our example above, you would choose to pay off the $5,000 loan first before tackling the $2,000 head-on. It's not always this simple, though. If you have many loans to pay off, they'll most likely be different balances at different interest rates. What method would you choose then?

If your utmost priority is to save money, it would be best to go with avalanche method. If your priority is to feel really good about shedding off debt one by one, the snowball method is best. My priority at the start of my journey was to pay off my debts as quickly as possible, while saving on interest. Especially with the fact that it compounds. (Compound interest is the interest charged on the interest charged on your principal - the horror!) This led me to combine both snowball and avalanche methods - I call this the hybrid method.

For example, I would do an equal payment split between two loans, regardless of their interest rates. If I had a $4,000 loan at 5% interest and a $5,000 loan at 4% interest, I would put all my efforts into both at the same time. If I had a third $10,000 loan at 20% interest, I would use the avalanche method to pay this off first, before putting equal efforts in the other two debts. If I had a $1,000 loan with 0% interest, I would rather put my $1,000 towards the other loans, then pay off the $1,000 loan after paying off the rest. I did what made sense to me. So, you do what makes sense to you. As long as the loans are getting paid, that's what matters.

Here's a scenario:

Ashley lives in Melbourne, Australia. Her freelance writing gig and corporate job nets her an income of $6,000 per month after tax. She decides that 35% of this will go towards her debt repayment (35% x $6,000 = $2,500). To her, 35% is very high but she is willing to do this as she wants to pay off her debt faster. She chooses to do this using the snowball method, meaning that she will pay off the debt with the least principal first while paying the minimum payment or slightly higher)on her other debts. She has a $6,000 student loan at 4% interest and a $10,000 car loan at 6%. She wants to pay them off in 88 months.

After inputting her numbers on a credit card calculator she found online (moneysmart.gov.au credit-cards credit-card-calculator), she knows that she will pay off her student loan in four months if she pays approximately$2,000 towards this loan per month (total interest will be $20). During these four months, she was also paying the remaining $100 towards her car loan. After she cleared her student loan, she then put all $2,100 towards her car loan. She was able to pay this off in the subsequent four months. After eight months since her journey began, Ashley is debt-free.

What does your debt repayment plan look like? How fast do you want it paid off? I'm not the greatest mathematician in the world, so I find debt repayment calculators to be super helpful. Find a calculator online, input your numbers on the MFP budget tracker and watch your debt reduce month by month.

Tracking Investment and Savings Payments

Now let's discuss the second section. See example, using the budget tracker, on the next page.

TRACKING INVESTMENT AND SAVINGS PAYMENTS

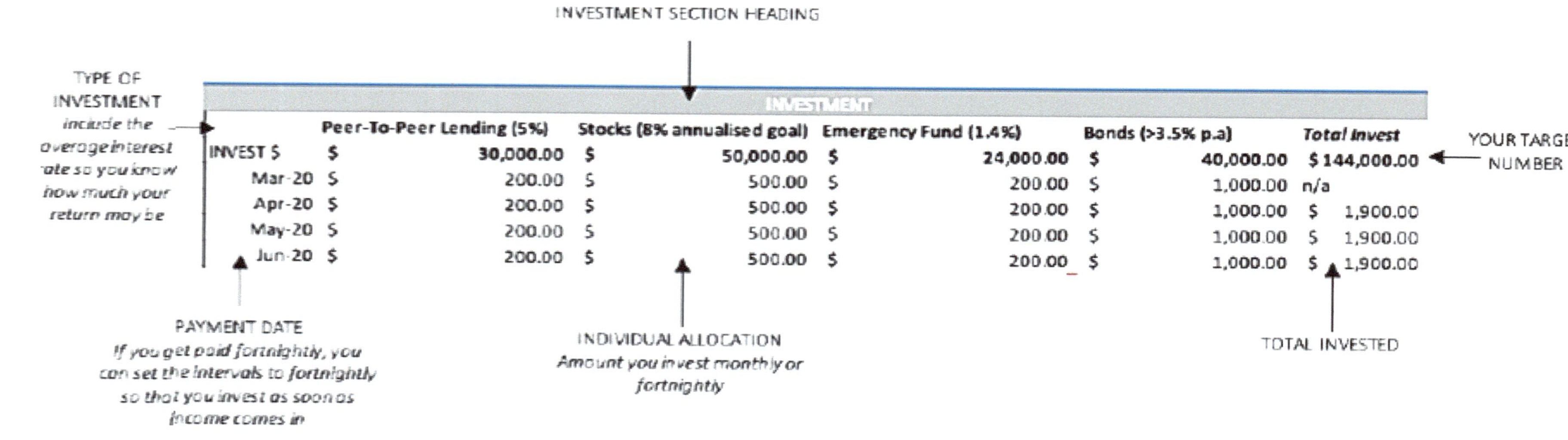

INVESTMENT					
	Peer-To-Peer Lending (5%)	Stocks (8% annualised goal)	Emergency Fund (1.4%)	Bonds (>3.5% p.a)	*Total Invest*
INVEST $	**$ 30,000.00**	**$ 50,000.00**	**$ 24,000.00**	**$ 40,000.00**	**$ 144,000.00**
Mar-20	$ 200.00	$ 500.00	$ 200.00	$ 1,000.00	n/a
Apr-20	$ 200.00	$ 500.00	$ 200.00	$ 1,000.00	$ 1,900.00
May-20	$ 200.00	$ 500.00	$ 200.00	$ 1,000.00	$ 1,900.00
Jun-20	$ 200.00	$ 500.00	$ 200.00	$ 1,000.00	$ 1,900.00

Just as you've done in the Debt Repayment section, do the following in chronological order:

- Decide on a percentage you can contribute towards Investment/ Savings. How much from your Gross Income can you afford to allocate? 10%? 20%? 30%? What amount is this?

- List out the types of investments and savings goal you'd like to work towards. For example, emergency fund (from Step 3), wedding, child's college fund, vacation, brand new car, first home, stocks (self-managed and/or retirement accounts such as 401k, Super, Kiwisaver), bonds, and so on.

- Spread these goals across five years by asking yourself: How much would I like to have in [*name of goal*]] in five years?

- Then, break up each goal's 5-year figure per month. The total of your per month should equal to the percentage you chose to allocate to Investment/Savings.

Every month that you contribute to your portfolio takes you one step closer to your five-year goal.

Investing is a whole different ball game. So, before you embark on any new investment plan, please get informed. I can't stress this enough. Read on the topic, watch tons of videos, take a course, get a mentor that's been successful in the craft, or speak with a licensed financial advisor. One of the greatest investors of our time, Warren Buffett, advises to only invest in things we *understand.*

Whatever investment options you're interested in, whether it's bonds, the stock market, cryptocurrency, peer-to-peer lending, precious metals, real estate, venture capitalism, you name it, you've got to understand it. Investing can either make or break you, but you can manage your risk if you're well-informed.

Finally, remember that the Emergency Fund is not there to make you money. Its purpose is not to be an "investment" in the financial sense of the word, but a life raft in the event of a tide!

YOUR NOTES

What type of investments (or savings goal) are you interested in or already have? How much can you (or do you) put towards each on a regular basis?

....

....

....

....

....

....

....

....

STEP 7: HAVE ANNUAL MILESTONES TO REACH

Five years might seem like a long time to achieve your money goals. The wins couldn't come fast enough! So, it's handy to break these bigger goals down to milestones. Write out SMART milestones that you would like to hit by the end of each year. It could be debt-related, investment-related or savings-related.

Here is an example:

- [[January 2021]] Save $2,000 in emergency fund by December 2021
- [[January 2022]] Pay off at least $10,000 in student loan by December 2020
- [[January 2023]] Pay off car loan by December 2023
- [[January 2024]] Have a $50,000 deposit on my first home by December 2024
- [[January 2025]] Contribute $20,000 to my retirement fund by December 2025

As you can see, these goals are Specific (one focused goal per year), Measurable (you have a payment plan in place from Step 6), Attainable (you have modelled these based on the realistic monthly/fortnightly payment plan), Relevant (these are your desires), and Timely (December, YEAR).

I actually placed my personal yearly goals at the very top of my budget tracker so I'm always reminded of what my top priority is on my money journey.

What would you like to achieve by the end of this year? Write it down and track your progress!

YOUR NOTES

What five key yearly milestones you would like to achieve?

YEAR: ....

MILESTONE: ....

YEAR: ....

MILESTONE: ....

YEAR: ....

MILESTONE: ....

YEAR: ....

MILESTONE: ....

YEAR: ....

MILESTONE: ....

STEP 8: CELEBRATE YOUR MILESTONES

Have you now crafted a sound and realistic budget with yearly goals for yourself? Congratulations! You have just set a clear path for yourself and your financial future. Happy days!

This step is another one dear to my heart. Humour me as I use an example of a TikTok trend called #FruitSnackChallenge to illustrate my point. There's a particular challenge trending on the social media app, TikTok, that requires a parent to film themselves placing a bowl of goodies in front of their child, asking the child not to touch it until they get back. The parent cleverly leaves the child's vicinity and we, the viewers, watch to see if the child will reach for the sweets or not. I mean, you might as well take the kid to Willy Wonka's Chocolate Factory (from 1971's film, *Willy Wonka and the Chocolate Factory))* and ask them not to eat any chocolate...

In some of the #FruitSnackChallenge videos, the child is patient and does not touch the sweets until the parent comes back (This is the kind of patience I aspire to have!). In other videos, the child couldn't resist and they give in to the temptation. Now, imagine if we change the rules. The parents tell their children (specifically, the older ones) that if they don't reach for the sweets, they'll go to Disneyland for Christmas. I can imagine there'd be more children exercising patience and willpower! In this scenario, the reward outweighs the struggle. This is delayed gratification in action.

Human beings thrive on rewards. We want to get recognised for our efforts. And, it starts with recognising ourselves. As I keep saying throughout this e-book, the journey to wealth is not easy. We have to exercise patience like the kid who's promised Disneyland at Christmas. It's a hustle which I know you're ready for - I mean, you got this far! But, during this hustle, remember to reward yourself for every major achievement.

Human beings thrive on rewards. We want to get recognised for our efforts. And, it starts with recognising ourselves.

AUTHOR'S NOTE

It could be something as small as buying a bottle of your favourite French wine or getting the most expensive beauty treatment on the list, to something as big as buying a fancy gadget or piece of furniture you've had on your wish list for so long. It could be getting an expensive bedding set or painting your room. Whatever it is, it should make you feel good and rewarded.

Where's the money going to come from? It could be from your sinking fund or your net income. We haven't really talked much about the sinking fund so far. That's because it's optional.

A sinking fund is basically a back-up savings fund. The 'sinking fund' is a term most used in business whereby the company or management saves for a rainy day or to pay off existing debt. It's like their version of an emergency fund or a savings account. If we apply this concept to our own personal lives, a sinking fund can then be a backup savings fund.

For me, the emergency fund is mandatory, but a sinking fund is not. We need emergency funds for emergencies, especially high-cost emergencies. If there was a situation where I needed a small amount of money to solve a problem, I would generally take it out of my net income. Moreover, I don't need to save up to pay my debts as I pay it on a monthly basis as a percentage of my income (as per the MFP tracker). So, I personally don't use a sinking fund. But, you can if you want this extra backup savings fund, especially for things like rewarding yourself.

FORTUNE DOES FAVOR THE BOLD, AND YOU'LL NEVER KNOW WHAT YOU'RE CAPABLE OF IF YOU DON'T TRY.

SHERYL SANDBERG
CHIEF OPERATING OFFICER, *FACEBOOK*

STEP 9: INCREASE YOUR INCOME

If you want to accelerate your financial goals, the most effective way is to simply make more money. The more you have coming in, the more you have to allocate to your debts, savings, and investments. Some people may just want to build wealth with their main source of income, and that's perfectly fine. The only thing is that it may just take longer. Compare the person who budgets using one source of income and another who budgets using two or more. Who has the advantage of reaching their goals faster? The one with more sources of income, of course.

I ve always been entrepreneurial by nature. My grandmother was a primary school teacher by trade, but she was also a seamstress, arts and craft maker, farmer, and retail shop owner. She made a decent amount from these, whilst raising six children and two grandchildren (me included). My grandfather was also very industrial, and this definitely did not skip a generation: my parents went down the same path, even with a day job.

If you want to accelerate your financial goals, the most effective way is to simply make more money.

AUTHOR'S NOTE

Everyone can be industrious. We all have something to offer the world. You may have a talent or skill that you can teach others. You may have knowledge on a topic that you can share with those who seek it, just like I m doing now with this e-book. You can teach others something you are passionate about and make some extra income on the side.

Think of two top things you're good at, and find ways to monetise them. You can become a freelancer, start a YouTube channel, start a blog, hold local courses, write a book, the possibilities are endless! Or, you could do things for people. Are you good at cleaning? Painting? Organising closets?Proofreading and editing? Audio recording? Film editing? Singing? Public speaking? Counselling/ coaching? Playing an instrument? Hair styling?People will pay you to make their lives easier and feel happier. Search online for service provider websites like Airtasker or Fiverr and create a profile. Put yourself out there and watch what happens.

Perhaps you're saying to yourself, *"But I'm not sure of what I'm good at".* First of all, I'm sure there is *something* you're good at. Otherwise, learn something new and teach it to others. It may take a few months to get really good at it, but it's a worthy investment. Another way is to basically turn anything you have into an asset. Car? Rent it out. Space? Rent it out. Clothes? Rent it out. I've done many a side gig in my life, and still continue to do so, and it has definitely moved my goals forward.

Aside from side gigs, you can also start a business. I urge you to be careful with this one, though, because solid businesses almost always need funding. If you have a lot of debt presently, I suggest you go to the side gig route first before starting a full-scale business. You might just spot an opportunity down the line to turn your successful side gig into a business!

Brainstorm ways you can monetise 1 key talent/skill/knowledge you have

SKILL/TALENT/KNOWLEDGE:

....

I CAN MAKE MONEY WITH THIS BY:

....

....

....

....

MY RELATIONSHIP WITH MONEY IS THAT IT'S A TOOL TO BE SELF-SUFFICIENT, BUT IT'S NOT SOMETHING THAT IS A PART OF WHO I AM.

LAURENE POWELL JOBS
FOUNDER, *EMERSON COLLECTIVE*

STEP 10: HAVE FUN AND DON'T STARVE YOURSELF

You made it to the final step! Well done!

How do you feel about the steps so far? Are you intrigued? Are you inspired? Are you up for the challenge? I truly hope so. From my corner of the world in Sydney, do know that I am supporting you. I am rooting for you. At this point, you should now be equipped and energised to start being intentional with your finances. You will no longer serve money, money will serve you. This final step is about being mindful throughout your journey, so let's begin.

Health is wealth. We've heard this many times. If you're super disciplined on your journey, you will be tempted many times to put your goals first before your health. Don't give into this. Putting our health second can mean a lot of things, no matter how trivial. It could be opting for fast food meal just because it's cheaper over gourmet, or avoiding the pharmacy when you're sick because you don't want to spend $50 on medicine.

You probably think it's odd I'm talking about this. But, this journey you're on is long-term. And when you become so aware of how much you could save in some situations, you may just put your health second. We don't want that.

Money is simply the means to an end, not the end itself. Our priorities should be the intangible things we count as most important to us - family, connections, friendships, moments, faith, the list goes on. *Health* should be on that list as well.

So, when I say "don't starve yourself", I'm not only talking about food and nutrition. I'm also talking about the things that are important to you. Stay enriched. Have fun. When you do this, your financial journey will be nothing short of *wholesome*.

CLOSING THOUGHTS

*"What if my income is suddenly dramatically reduced? What happens to my plan then?** you might ask.

As at the time of writing this e-book, the whole world is in the middle of a Coronavirus pandemic. Our world has changed so rapidly within a short period of time. Many employees have had their hours reduced, including myself, while others have been let go. Small business owners are either having to close up shop or operate at a loss, albeit temporarily, with limited capacity. It's a morbid situation, and my prayers go out to those who have been affected by the pandemic.

In situations where your income is dramatically reduced, you simply re-adjust your percentages. Here's how I have readjusted mine to work at this time:

	BEFORE	**AFTER**
Gross Income	Complete	Halved
Monthly Bills	34%	45%
Debt Repayment	38%	30%
Savings/Investments	14%	10%
Net Income	15%	15%

I adjusted my percentages to suit me. I've also kept my debt repayment relatively high because I am determined to achieve my focused goal for the year (Step 7 in action). The majority of my new Savings/Investments money is going towards my Emergency Fund. Your Emergency Fund is even more important at such a time like this. So is paying off any high interest rate debts you may have. Nobody knows what tomorrow holds, but whatever it does hold, you'll be glad you prepared today.

As a reader, it's only natural to have questions as you embark on your own money journey. The good news, though, is that you are not alone. I created the *Sisters with a Plan* blog in the hopes of answering your questions. On the blog, you will find informative and actionable content that will help you on your journey towards financial freedom.

Sisters with a Plan was created to encourage and nurture the community of women everywhere seeking financial freedom. Through the blog and future platforms in the works, we can bounce ideas off one another, encourage each other, and share our successes and challenges. I look forward to having you there! If you have anything you'd like me to share with the community or you have any other questions, please feel free email me at keji.adebeshin@gmail.com. I'd love to hear from you.

Time is one thing we can't get back. The time you spend paying down debt and investing in your future is time well-spent. Rome may not have been built in a day, but it only took a brick to start. The desire was there, the drive was there, and its builders maintained momentum till it became the city we know it as today. Apply this to your own money journey. And, once you achieve your ultimate goal - freedom, sweet, sweet freedom, you will thank your past self for laying that first brick today.

That's all in a nutshell! I hope you enjoyed this e-book! If so, why don't you head over to sisterswithaplan.com or Amazon to leave a review for others. Your opinion is very much appreciated.

Also, stay tuned for a follow-up e-book on the art of EARNING money. When you know how to earn additional income outside of your day job and investments, whether it be from side gigs or starting a business, you can achieve your money goals even quicker.

I'll leave you with this Chinese proverb:

The best time to plant a tree was 20 years ago. The second-best time is now.

www.sisterswithaplan.com

www.ingramcontent.com/pod-product-compliance
Lightning Source LLC
LaVergne TN
LVHW071124160826
845679LV00005B/1172

* 9 7 9 8 6 6 5 1 5 2 1 6 5 *